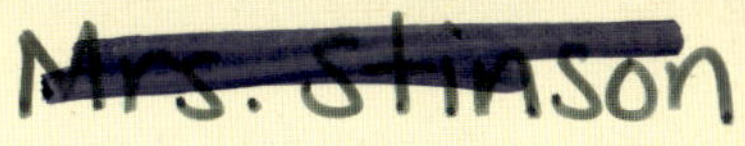

The Friendly Beasts

Illustrated by John J. Blumen

Adapted by Karen L. Blumen

Augsburg
MINNEAPOLIS

Music and complete lyrics appear on pages 30 and 31.

THE FRIENDLY BEASTS

Cover and interior design: Elizabeth Boyce

Blumen, John, 1954–
The friendly beasts / illustrated by John J. Blumen ; adapted by Karen L. Blumen.
p. cm.
Summary: An old English Christmas carol in which the friendly stable beasts tell of the gifts which they have given to the newborn Child.
ISBN 0-8066-3330-1
1. Carols, English—England—Texts. 2. Christmas music—Texts. [1. Carols—England. 2. Christmas music.] I. Blumen, Karen, 1954– ill. II. Title.
PZ8.3.B59864Fr 1997 97-28193
782.28'1723—dc21 CIP
[E] AC

The paper used in this publication meets the minimum requirements of American National Standard for Information Sciences—Permanence of Paper for Printed Library Materials, ANSI Z329.48-1984. ∞

Printed in Hong Kong AF 9-3330

01 00 99 98 97 1 2 3 4 5 6 7 8 9 10

Introduction

The Friendly Beasts is a wonderful story to share with children at Christmas! It's based on the familiar account of the birth of Christ that has been told for 2000 years and is known throughout the world. The biblical account of the journey of Mary and Joseph to Bethlehem, the birth of Jesus, and the visit of the shepherds is recorded in Luke 2:1-20, and the later visit of the Magi from the East appears in Matthew 2:1-12.

Before reading *The Friendly Beasts* to children, be sure they are familiar with the story of Jesus' birth. Then explain that *The Friendly Beasts* tells the story the way the animals who were there might have told it. Let young children find and identify each animal in the book before you read the text. They will love the exceptional illustrations and may wish to talk about many of the captivating details in the pictures. Explain that the first "friendly beasts" they meet are ones that could have been in the stable when Jesus was born, followed by the shepherds' and Wise Men's animals, and finally the field mice.

Children often worry at Christmastime that they have no money with which to purchase gifts—no "real gifts" to give. As you read this story discuss the importance of each animal's gift apart from monetary cost. From the camels' rich gifts of spices and gold to the heart-felt offering of "love most true" from the field mice, each animal gives its best to the baby Jesus, and each gift is priceless. May this story about the friendly beasts help your child realize that he or she, too, has wonderful gifts to give!

Jesus, our brother, kind and good,
Humbly was born in a stable of wood;

And the friendly beasts around him stood,
Jesus, our brother, kind and good.

"I," said the donkey, shaggy and brown,
"Carried his mother uphill and down;
I bore his mother to Bethlehem town,
I," said the donkey, shaggy and brown.

"I," said the cow, all white and red,
"Gave him my manger for his bed;
And offered my hay to pillow his head,
I," said the cow, all white and red.

"I," said the dove from rafters high,
"Cooed him to sleep so he would not cry;
We lulled him to sleep, my mate and I,
I," said the dove from rafters high.

"I," said the cat with velvet fur,
"Curled at his feet and for him did purr;
Warming his toes so he need not stir,
I," said the cat with velvet fur.

“I,” said the spider on silken line,
“Wove him a halo to be a sign;
He’ll be the Savior to thee and thine,
I,” said the spider on silken line.

“I,” said the sheep with curly horn,
“Gave him my wool for a blanket warm;
He wore my coat on Christmas morn,
I,” said the sheep with curly horn.

“I,” said the dog from neighboring farm,
“Kept our sweet babe from every harm;
At any strange noise, I barked in alarm,
I,” said the dog from neighboring farm.

"We," said the camels, travelers bold,
"Followed the star that was foretold;
Bearing his gifts of spices and gold,
We," said the camels, travelers bold.

"We," said the mice, the poorest of you,
"Offered to him our love most true;
This gift the greatest of all that we knew,
We," said the mice, the poorest of you.

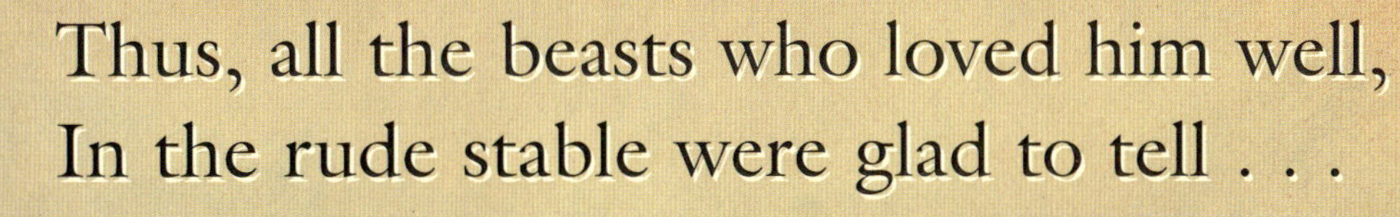

Thus, all the beasts who loved him well,
In the rude stable were glad to tell . . .

Of the gifts they gave to Emmanuel,
Of the gifts they gave to Emmanuel.

The Friendly Beasts

The tune for *The Friendly Beasts* is a thirteenth century French carol called "Oriental Partibus," which was sung for the famous medieval Christmas festival Fete de L'Ane in Beauvois, France. The tune was revived by Richard Redhead, the great British hymnist, during the 1850s. In the early 1900s Robert Davis, one-time assistant minister of Brick Presbyterian Church in New York, wrote *The Friendly Beasts* to the accompaniment of "Oriental Partibus" for a Christmas pageant by Dr. Clarence Dickenson. His six original verses have been adapted slightly, and an additional five verses have been added for this book.

The Friendly Beasts

Complete lyrics

1. Jesus, our brother, kind and good,
Humbly was born in a stable of wood;
And the friendly beasts around him stood,
Jesus, our brother, kind and good.

2. "I," said the donkey, shaggy and brown,
"Carried his mother uphill and down;
I bore his mother to Bethlehem town,
I," said the donkey, shaggy and brown.

3. "I," said the cow, all white and red,
"Gave him my manger for his bed;
And offered my hay to pillow his head,
I," said the cow, all white and red.

4. "I," said the dove from rafters high,
"Cooed him to sleep so he would not cry;
We lulled him to sleep, my mate and I,
I," said the dove from rafters high.

5. "I," said the cat with velvet fur,
"Curled at his feet and for him did purr;
Warming his toes so he need not stir,
I," said the cat with velvet fur.

6. "I," said the spider on silken line,
"Wove him a halo to be a sign;
He'll be the Savior to thee and thine,
I," said the spider on silken line.

7. "I," said the sheep with curly horn,
"Gave him my wool for a blanket warm;
He wore my coat on Christmas morn,
I," said the sheep with curly horn.

8. "I," said the dog from neighboring farm,
"Kept our sweet babe from every harm;
At any strange noise, I barked in alarm,
I," said the dog from neighboring farm.

9. "We," said the camels, travelers bold,
"Followed the star that was foretold;
Bearing his gifts of spices and gold,
We," said the camels, travelers bold.

10. "We," said the mice, the poorest of you,
"Offered to him our love most true;
This gift the greatest of all that we knew,
We," said the mice, the poorest of you.

11. Thus, all the beasts who loved him well,
In the rude stable were glad to tell
Of the gifts they gave to Emmanuel,
Of the gifts they gave to Emmanuel.

Family Activities

Children will love to hear, read, tell, or sing the story of *The Friendly Beasts* again and again. Here are some related activities they may also enjoy:

- Role-play the story. Let each family member pretend to be a different animal and enter the action at the appropriate time. If possible, let each "animal" sing his or her verse of the song.

- Ask younger children to count all the animals in the story and then identify which are big animals, which are small, and which are in between; which have two legs, four legs, eight legs, wings. Let them portray each animal kinesthetically and vocally by showing how it moves and by making the sounds it uses for communication.

- Help children make clay or paper animals to add to your Christmas creche. Let them assist in making and stringing animal cookies or animal ornaments on the tree, or creating a Christmas "friendly beasts" table decoration.

- Compare the animals and sequence of events in *The Friendly Beasts* to the biblical accounts of the birth of Jesus in Luke 2:1-20, and Matthew 2:1-12.

- Let children illustrate their own collection of friendly beasts on blank pages, which later can be stapled into a book. Encourage them to draw themselves plus additional animals and show the gifts each brings.